TIMELINES

The War in Afghanistan

Brian Williams

FRANKLIN WATTS
LONDON•SYDNEY

First published in 2010 by Franklin Watts

Copyright © 2010 Arcturus Publishing Limited

Franklin Watts
338 Euston Road
London NW1 3BH

Franklin Watts Australia
Level 17/207 Kent Street, Sydney, NSW 2000

Produced by Arcturus Publishing Limited,
26/27 Bickels Yard, 151–153 Bermondsey Street, London SE1 3HA

Series concept: Alex Woolf
Editor and picture researcher: Nicola Barber
Consultant: James Vaughan
Designer: Ariadne Ward
Illustrator: Stefan Chabluk

Picture credits:
Corbis: cover (epa), 5 (Reuters), 7 (Reza/Webistan), 8 (Pascal Manoukian/Sygma), 9 (Patrick Robert/Sygma), 10 (Patrick Robert/Sygma), 15 (Reuters), 19 (Reuters), 20 (Reuters), 21 (Danny Rose/epa), 22 (Reza/Webistan), 23 (Ed Darack/Science Faction), 24 (Reuters), 25 (Stringer/Afghanistan/Reuters), 26 (Ahmad Masood/Reuters), 27 (Ahmad Masood/Reuters), 28 (Ahmad Masood/Reuters), 29 (Larry Downing/Reuters), 30 (David Bathgate), 31 (David Bathgate), 35 (STR/epa), 36 (Humayoun Shiab/epa), 37 (T Mughal/epa), 38 (Mohsin Raza/Reuters), 39 (T Mughal/epa), 40 (Humayoun Shiab/epa), 41 (Marvin B Moore/USAF/US Department of Defense/NSArchive.org/Reuters), 42 (Stringer/epa), 43 (Humayoun Shiab/epa), 44 (Pete Souza/White House/Handout/CNP), 45 (Rashid Iqbal/epa).
Rex Features: 6 (Sipa Press), 11 (Sipa Press), 12 (Charles Sykes), 13 (Ron Sachs), 14 (Peter Nicholls), 16 (Sipa Press), 17 (Sipa Press), 18, 32 (Action Press), 33 (Sipa Press), 34 (Nick Cornish).
Cover picture: Taliban fighters photographed in Helmand province, 2008.

A CIP catalogue record for this book is available from the British Library.

Dewey Decimal Classification Number: 958.1'047

ISBN 978 0 7496 9537 8

Printed in China

Franklin Watts is a division of Hachette Children's Books, an Hachette UK company.
www.hachette.co.uk

Contents

▷ A New Nation – 8 August 1919   **4**

▷ The Soviet Invasion – 24 December 1979   **6**

▷ Holy Warriors – 15 February 1989   **8**

▷ Opposing the Taliban – 10 October 1996   **10**

▷ Attack on America – 11 September 2001   **12**

▷ Operation Enduring Freedom – 7 October 2001   **14**

▷ Northern Alliance Triumphs – 9 November 2001   **16**

▷ The Hunt for Bin Laden – 16 December 2001   **18**

▷ Guantánamo Bay – 11 January 2002   **20**

▷ New Leadership – 13 June 2002   **22**

▷ Assassination Target – 5 September 2002   **24**

▷ NATO Takes Command – 11 August 2003   **26**

▷ Elections and Terror Attacks – 9 October 2004   **28**

▷ Helicopter Down – 28 June 2005   **30**

▷ Operation Mountain Thrust – 15 May 2006   **32**

▷ Operation Achilles – 6 March 2007   **34**

▷ Murder and Suicide Bombs – 17 February 2008   **36**

▷ Cross-Border Raids – 10 June 2008   **38**

▷ Prison Break and Tensions – 13 June 2008   **40**

▷ Civilians Under Attack – 22 August 2008   **42**

▷ An Exit Strategy? – 23 March 2009   **44**

▷ Key Figures in the War in Afghanistan   **46**

▷ Glossary   **47**

▷ Further Information   **47**

▷ Index   **48**

A New Nation

8 AUGUST 1919

In August 1919, Afghanistan became a newly independent nation. For 2,000 years it had been a target for foreign invaders, from Alexander the Great (300s BCE) to Genghis Khan (1200s CE). From the 1500s to the 1700s, Afghanistan was part of the Moguls' great Indian empire. In the 19th century, Afghanistan became a strategic chess piece in the 'Great Game' – a term often used to describe the rivalry between Britain and Russia for control of Central Asia. Britain, which then ruled India, fought two wars against Afghanistan, in 1838 and 1878. The Treaty of Rawalpindi (8 August 1919) ended a third war between the two countries. Under the terms of the treaty Britain recognized the independence of Afghanistan, and most Afghans looked forward to a more peaceful and prosperous future. Theirs was a poor country and one that was ready, some thought, for modernization.

Afghanistan is a rugged, landlocked country with an area of 647,500 sq km.

MODERNIZERS VS CONSERVATIVES

Modernizing rulers trod a dangerous path in Afghanistan. In 1933, Zahir became shah (king) after the murder of his father, Nadir Shah. Zahir Shah introduced reforms but Afghan society remained conservative; real power

The people of Afghanistan

Afghanistan has a population of about 32 million. Kabul is the capital and biggest city. Other major cities are Kandahar, Herat and Mazar-e Sharif. The population is largely rural – 78 per cent of Afghans live in villages. Almost all Afghans are Muslims – over 75 per cent Sunni, the rest Shia. Pashtuns make up almost half the population; other large ethnic groups are Tajiks (18 per cent), Hazaras (9 per cent) and Uzbeks (8 per cent). The official languages are Pashto and Dari (an Iranian dialect).

| TIMELINE | **ROAD TO A REPUBLIC 1893–1973** |

1893 ▶	The Durand Line agreement fixes the border between Afghanistan and British India.
20 February 1919 ▶	Assassination of the pro-British Habibullah Khan; his (anti-British) third son Amanullah becomes Afghanistan's ruler.
May 1919 ▶	Third war between Afghanistan and Britain, during which British aircraft bomb Kabul.
8 August 1919 ▶	Treaty of Rawalpindi: Britain recognizes Afghanistan's independence.
January 1929 ▶	Amanullah, a reformer, steps down as shah (king). Nadir Khan becomes shah in October 1929.
8 November 1933 ▶	Assassination of Nadir Shah; his son Zahir succeeds him at the age of 19.
17 July 1973 ▶	Daud Khan declares Afghanistan a republic.

lay with the Islamic religious leaders and the chiefs of the country's tribal and ethnic groups. In 1973, Daud Khan, a former prime minister (1953–63), made the country a republic and Zahir Shah went into exile.

DAUD'S BALANCING ACT

Daud was a Pashtun, the dominant ethnic group in Afghanistan. United by language (Pashto) and a clan (extended family) system, Pashtuns live on both sides of the Afghanistan-Pakistan border. Daud wanted to modernize, and sought help from the communist Soviet Union. At the same time he looked for friends and aid from Islamic nations and the West. This tricky balancing act upset both conservative tribal leaders and radicals who believed Afghanistan's problems could be solved only by revolution.

CROSS-REFERENCE THE SOVIET INVASION: PAGES 6–7

A Pashtun fighter with a rocket-propelled grenade. Pashtun people make up Afghanistan's largest ethnic group.

The Soviet Invasion

24 DECEMBER 1979

On 24 December 1979, the Soviet leader Leonid Brezhnev sent Soviet troops to prop up the communist government in Afghanistan. Afghanistan had become a pawn in the Cold War, a power struggle between the Soviet Union (USSR) and the United States. However the invasion of Afghanistan was to become the Soviets' 'Vietnam' – a war they could not win.

Russian tanks move into Kabul in 1979. Soviet troops and Afghan soldiers loyal to Babrak Kamal took over key government buildings.

COMMUNIST REVOLUTION

Afghanistan was one of the first countries to recognize the communist Soviet Union after the revolution in Russia in 1917. President Daud, who continued this friendship, was also an advocate of 'Pashtunistan', uniting Pashtuns on both sides of the Afghanistan-Pakistan border in some form of separate state. This prospect antagonized both the Pakistan government and non-Pashtun ethnic groups such as the Tajiks of northern Afghanistan. Daud made more enemies among Afghan radicals, who wanted revolution. In April 1978 he was overthrown by a trio of enemies: Hafizullah Amin, Babrak Kamal and Nur Mohammad Taraki. Taraki led a new hardline communist government,

Cold War rivalry

The Cold War began in the 1940s as the world's two superpowers, the United States and the Soviet Union, vied for supremacy. Both superpowers had nuclear weapons and massive armed forces. The Americans tried to hold back the spread of communism – which is why they became involved in the Korean War (1950s) and the Vietnam War (1960s–70s). The Soviets controlled Eastern Europe, sent aid to revolutionary Cuba, and tried to get control of Afghanistan. The two Cold War rivals avoided direct military action against each other; instead they carried on a secret war of spying, subversion and regional conflicts.

COUNTDOWN TO THE SOVIET INVASION 1978–1979

27 April 1978	President Daud is killed as communists seize power in a bloody revolution.
14 February 1979	The US ambassador, Adolph Dubs, is murdered in Kabul.
20 March 1979	President Taraki visits Moscow to ask for Soviet aid.
10 October 1979	Taraki's death is reported in Kabul; mystery surrounds the circumstances.
24 December 1979	President Amin is overthrown; Soviet troops seize Kabul airport and move across Afghanistan's northern border.

which brought in laws to redistribute land, end forced marriages and challenge Muslim sharia law. His reforms provoked a fierce reaction, and tribal resistance leaders began fighting the government.

THE SOVIETS MOVE IN

By early 1979 the Taraki regime was in serious trouble. As violence escalated, the US ambassador to Afghanistan, Adolph Dubs, was kidnapped in Kabul. He died in a gunfight between his captors and the Afghan security forces, who were helped by Soviet secret agents. The United States protested at the Soviet involvement, but Taraki turned to the USSR for more assistance. Taraki was overthrown in October 1979; it was reported that he died after an illness, but he was almost certainly murdered. His successor, Hafizullah Amin, was killed in December and the Soviets installed Babrak Kamal as president. At the same time they sent in thousands of combat troops. A new Afghan war had started.

CROSS-REFERENCE
THE 'GREAT GAME':
PAGES 4–5
THE BATTLE AGAINST
THE SOVIETS:
PAGES 8–9

Bill Richardson, US ambassador to the UN, at the grave of Adolph Dubs in 1998. The death of a diplomat in Kabul revealed how Afghan internal security was deteriorating in 1979.

Holy Warriors

Young mujahideen fighters with a captured Soviet vehicle. Both the US Central Intelligence Agency (CIA) and Pakistan's security agency, the Inter-Services Intelligence (ISI), supplied weapons to the mujahideen to fight the Soviet army.

On 15 February 1989, the Soviet army left Afghanistan. About 15,000 Soviet soldiers were dead; Afghan losses were as high as 100,000, yet after nine years the Soviets had failed to defeat the anti-communist rebels, known as the mujahideen ('holy warriors').

THE MUJAHIDEEN

The mujahideen was a collection of resistance groups. Two of the most powerful of these groups were Jamiat-e Islami ('Islamic Society'), led by Burhanuddin Rabbani and Ahmad Shah Massoud, and the Taliban ('students of religious law'), led by Mullah Mohammed Omar. The mainly Pashtun Taliban imposed strict Islamic religious law on the territory it controlled. The mujahideen welcomed foreign Muslim fighters, including Osama bin Laden. Money and weapons for the mujahideen came from Pakistan, China, Iran, Saudi Arabia, Israel – and the United States, which was eager to thwart Soviet policy whenever it could.

END OF COMMUNIST RULE

During the war millions of refugees had fled to Iran and Pakistan. Both these countries were important allies of the mujahideen. In 1986, Afghanistan's President Kamal was replaced by another communist, Mohammad Najibullah. By then, the Soviet Union also had a new leader, Mikhail Gorbachev. In February 1986, Gorbachev spoke of Afghanistan as a 'bleeding wound'. In the following year, Gorbachev decided to put an end to a war in which the Soviet army had lost 15,000 dead and 37,000 wounded, and which was costing the USSR around

CROSS-REFERENCE
OPPOSING THE
TALIBAN:
PAGES 10–11

TIMELINE

SOVIET WITHDRAWAL AND CIVIL WAR 1985–1992

11 March 1985 ▶ Mikhail Gorbachev takes over as Soviet leader.

4 May 1986 ▶ Kamal is replaced as Afghanistan's president by Najibullah.

20 July 1987 ▶ Gorbachev announces Soviet troop withdrawals, to begin in 1988.

15 February 1989 ▶ The last Soviet troops leave Afghanistan.

April 1989 ▶ Talks in Geneva, Switzerland, between the various mujahideen groups fail to bring unity.

16 April 1992 ▶ Najibullah quits as president; with mujahideen groups fighting for control, he takes refuge in the United Nations compound in Kabul.

US$7.8 billion a year. But even after the last Soviet troops had finally left in 1989 Najibullah clung to power, fighting the mujahideen until 1992, when he resigned. Burhanuddin Rabbani was named as Afghanistan's new leader, but opposed by the Taliban. These events were watched from Pakistan by a new extremist group: al-Qaeda.

Afghans, some with pro-Soviet banners, watch Soviet troops pull out of Kabul in 1988. Uncertainty clouded Afghanistan's future.

Al-Qaeda

Al-Qaeda, Arabic for 'the base', was set up during 1988–89 by Osama bin Laden. Its aims were to remove 'corrupt regimes' in Muslim countries, and to get rid of Western influence. By the 1990s bin Laden had also turned his anger against the United States and Israel, which he blamed for the suffering of people in Palestine as a result of the Arab-Israeli conflict. Al-Qaeda has been accused of carrying out terror attacks worldwide from its base in Afghanistan, including the bombings of the US embassies in Kenya and Tanzania (1998), the suicide attack on USS *Cole* (2000), the 9/11 attacks on the United States (2001) and the London bombings (2005).

Opposing the Taliban

On 10 October 1996, various groups in the mujahideen came together to form a 'united Islamic front', known as the Northern Alliance, in a bid to halt a Taliban takeover. The alliance was dominated by minority ethnic groups (Tajiks, Uzbeks, Hazaras), and it was backed by Russia, India, Tajikistan, Uzbekistan, Iran and the United States. These nations had different views about what was best for Afghanistan, but they were united in their dislike of the Taliban.

TALIBAN TAKEOVER

After removing Najibullah in 1992, the mujahideen groups had begun to fight one another. In the bloodshed and confusion, and with no effective government, the way was open for a new force and a new leader: the Taliban, led by Mullah Mohammed Omar. The Taliban took over key cities such as Kandahar, and southern provinces such as Helmand. On 4 April 1996 they declared a jihad (holy war) against President Rabbani, and by September 1996 they had driven Rabbani from Kabul. Only three countries in the world, Pakistan, Saudi Arabia and the United Arab Emirates (UAE), recognized the Taliban as the new government of Afghanistan.

REPRESSION

Reports that came out of Afghanistan painted a grim picture of life under the Taliban: no music, no television, no non-Islamic books, no cinema. The religious police enforced severe punishments including beatings in the street, public executions and hand amputations (for stealing). The new laws were especially tough on women. Employment, education, travel, and easy access to hospitals were all forbidden. Women were obliged to cover themselves completely with a head-to-toe garment called a burka.

Ahmad Shah Massoud (hand raised) talks to fighters of the Northern Alliance. The experienced guerrilla leader drew support mainly from northern Afghanistan.

The Northern Alliance

The Northern Alliance was an army made up of different groups, mainly non-Pashtuns. Its best-known leader was Ahmad Shah Massoud, a Tajik from northern Afghanistan, known as the 'Lion of Panjshir'. Each group of fighters was loyal to its own generals including Mohammed Fahim Khan (Tajik), Abdul Rashid Dostum (Uzbek), Ismael Khan (Herat province) and Karim Khalili (Hazara). The leaders found it hard to work together. 'Political instability in [Afghanistan] is just what al-Qaeda and other extremist Islamic groups want', commented Pakistani writer Ahmed Rashid.

TIMELINE

TALIBAN RULE AND TERROR STRIKES 1996–2000

2 September 1996 ▶ Osama bin Laden calls on al-Qaeda supporters to fight 'infidels' (non-Muslims).

September 1996 ▶ Former president Najibullah is killed in Kabul.

7 August 1998 ▶ 224 people die when truck bombs blow up the US embassies in Kenya and Tanzania.

20 August 1998 ▶ US air strikes hit four terrorist camps in Afghanistan; bin Laden escapes.

6 February 2000 ▶ Peace talks between the Taliban and the Northern Alliance fail.

7 November 2000 ▶ George W Bush is elected president of the United States.

Girls were turned away from school. The Taliban also banned shaving (men had to grow beards), kite-flying (a favourite Afghan pastime), pigeon-keeping, gambling, Western hairstyles, money-changing for profit, washing clothes in rivers and dancing at weddings.

Under Taliban rule, women had to wear the burka. For many Muslims this was an alien and unwelcome imposition, but women had little choice but to conform.

BIN LADEN RETURNS

In May 1996, Osama bin Laden arrived back in Afghanistan after being expelled from Sudan. He had no previous public links with the Taliban, but he now received protection from the regime and made southern Afghanistan his base. In 1998 his al-Qaeda group launched two terror attacks on the US embassies in Nairobi (Kenya) and Dar es Salaam (Tanzania). The attacks killed 224 people. In retaliation, US President Bill Clinton authorized cruise missile strikes against suspected al-Qaeda camps in Sudan and Afghanistan. In 1999 the US Federal Bureau of Investigation (FBI) named bin Laden its 'most wanted terrorist'.

CROSS-REFERENCE
AL-QAEDA: PAGES 8–9
THE DEATH OF MASSOUD: PAGES 12–13
THE FIGHT AGAINST THE TALIBAN: PAGES 14–15

Attack on America

On 11 September 2001, US President George W Bush was visiting a school in Florida when shocking news came in. Two hijacked airliners had been flown into the World Trade Center, New York City; a third plane had hit the Pentagon, Washington, DC; a fourth had crashed in Pennsylvania. Almost 3,000 people died in the 9/11 attacks. On 14 September, the United States named Osama bin Laden as chief suspect.

MASSOUD'S MURDER

Two days before 9/11, the military commander of the Northern Alliance, Ahmad Shah Massoud, was assassinated in Afghanistan by two Tunisians. The assassins, posing as journalists, set off an explosive-packed camera. Although Rabbani was the official leader of the Northern Alliance, Massoud had become a key figure, and there was a clear link between his murder and 9/11. Intelligence reports suggested that his assassins were al-Qaeda killers, and that the order for Massoud's murder came directly from Osama bin Laden. By murdering Massoud, bin Laden hoped to win favour with the Taliban and to ensure their protection after 9/11 against the wrath of the United States.

THE WAR ON TERROR

America was stunned by the 9/11 attacks. President Bush spoke of a 'war on terror' and vowed to hit back. On 21 September, he told the US Congress, 'Whether we bring our enemies to justice, or bring justice to our enemies, justice will be done.' British Prime Minister Tony Blair pledged UK support, and rallied European nations to form a US-led international coalition to defeat al-Qaeda and the Taliban. The United States brought in new laws to hunt terrorists, and demanded that the Taliban hand over al-Qaeda leaders and close the camps allegedly used for terrorist training. When the Taliban

New York City is shrouded in dust as the towers of the World Trade Center collapse on 9/11. While millions of people around the world watched in horror as the events unfolded on television, the United States prepared to fight an unknown enemy.

CROSS-REFERENCE
MASSOUD AND THE
NORTHERN ALLIANCE:
PAGES 10–11
OPERATION
ENDURING FREEDOM:
PAGES 14–15

TIMELINE

THE WAR ON TERROR BEGINS 2001

9 September 2001
▶ Northern Alliance leader General Massoud is assassinated.

11 September 2001
▶ 9/11 attacks on America: an estimated 2,998 people are killed.

12 September 2001
▶ 19 countries of the North Atlantic Treaty Organization (NATO) promise support to the United States to fight the Taliban.

14 September 2001
▶ Taliban leader Mullah Omar says the Taliban will fight if attacked.

26 September 2001
▶ President Bush signs the Anti-Terrorism Act, giving the US government new powers to hunt terrorists.

refused, US and coalition forces prepared to attack Afghanistan. Refugees began heading out of Kabul in taxis, minibuses and trucks, and on foot. Jan Agha, a Pakistani student, told a Western journalist, 'The situation is deteriorating. It's really scary. It's not safe to go out at night for fear of being robbed or shot.'

President George W Bush and his wife attend a memorial service at the Pentagon for the people killed in the terrorist attacks of 9/11.

Bush vows vengeance

'We will pursue nations that provide aid or safe haven to terrorism. Every nation in every region has a decision to make: either you are with us or you are with the terrorists... This is the world's fight. This is civilization's fight. This is the fight of all who believe In progress and pluralism, tolerance and freedom. We ask every nation to join us.'
President Bush speaking to the US Congress, 21 September 2001.

Operation Enduring Freedom

Troops and equipment poured into Afghanistan, as Operation Enduring Freedom got under way. Smoke clouds show where coalition air strikes were hitting the Taliban.

On 7 October 2001, US and British forces attacked Taliban targets in Afghanistan. Other countries (including Australia, Canada, France and Germany) joined an international coalition. The Americans called the war on the Taliban 'Operation Enduring Freedom'. The Taliban had no diplomatic friends left; Pakistan, Saudi Arabia and the UAE all turned their backs, and Sudan, where Osama bin Laden had once been active, described itself as 'a party in the fight against terrorism'.

FIGHTING THE TALIBAN

Northern Alliance troops controlled Afghanistan north of Kabul. US warplanes flew from airfields in Tajikistan and

Afghanistan under attack

The coalition put a military ring around Afghanistan. Russia and India were neutral, but mostly supportive to the United States and its allies. Pakistan, bordering Afghanistan and with many Pashtuns among its population, was in a difficult situation. It could not afford to offend the United States, but it also had close links with the Taliban. Uzbekistan and Tajikistan allowed US forces to use their bases. Oman and the UAE also provided airfields. US aircraft carriers were in the Gulf and the Arabian Sea. B-1 and B-52 bombers flew from Diego Garcia, a British island used by the US navy in the Indian Ocean. Predator pilotless planes (drones) were controlled directly from the United States.

TIMELINE

OPENING HOSTILITIES 2001

7 October 2001 ▶ Air attacks begin on targets in Afghanistan.

16 October 2001 ▶ General Pervez Musharraf, leader of Pakistan since October 1999, agrees to help the USA fight terrorism.

19 October 2001 ▶ First US ground troops move into Afghanistan.

16 November 2001 ▶ Al-Qaeda military leader Mohammed Atef is killed by a missile launched from a US Predator drone.

Uzbekistan, and from aircraft carriers at sea. Missiles were fired from submarines, and B-2 bombers flew direct from the United States. The Taliban had few defences against such a massive air attack, and by October coalition ground troops were in action too.

The US navy provided air support for the forces in Afghanistan. These F-14 Tomcats flew from the carrier USS Theodore Roosevelt *in the Arabian Sea.*

TARGETING STRATEGY

The US government wanted to change Afghanistan's government ('regime change'), to arrest (or kill) Osama bin Laden and to destroy al-Qaeda. It was thought that bin Laden had masterminded several terrorist attacks before 9/11, including earlier attacks on the World Trade Center (1993), US embassy bombings in Africa (1998) and the attack on the warship USS *Cole* in Yemen (2000). The US military deployed special forces and aircraft to try to locate bin Laden. However, although an air strike by cruise missiles or unmanned aerial vehicles (UAVs; also known as 'smart bombs') can obliterate a target as small as a tent, it can kill innocent civilians too. Mistakes with the targeting of bombs can also result in their being misdirected. In 2002 alone there were between 3,000 and 5,000 Afghan casualties. US Defense Secretary Donald Rumsfeld defended the targeting strategy: 'we have approved every single target and each one is a military target'. But every civilian death fuelled the growing resentment among the Afghan people.

CROSS-REFERENCE PAKISTAN'S BALANCING ACT: PAGES 40–41

Northern Alliance Triumphs

On 9 November 2001, Northern Alliance troops led by the Uzbek commander Abdul Rashid Dostum captured the northern city of Mazar-e Sharif. By 14 November, the Taliban had been driven from Kabul, and in December they lost their last stronghold, Kandahar.

COLLAPSE OF THE TALIBAN

As Taliban power collapsed, Mullah Omar went into hiding while Osama bin Laden and other members of al-Qaeda were believed to be fugitives in the mountains. With the war 'won', Northern Alliance leaders discussed the make-up of a new government. Now that Massoud was dead, the alliance's most powerful leaders were Mohammed Fahim Khan, who led the Tajik fighters, and Dostum. US commanders waited to see who would lead Afghanistan, without really knowing much about the country and its complex groupings. Some hoped a Western-style democracy would quickly emerge. The Taliban had been driven from the cities but seemed to have vanished into the mountains and villages. Might there soon be a new guerrilla war, this time against the Americans?

PRISONERS AND DETAINEES

'War is our best hobby; the sound of guns firing is like music to us,' claimed Maulana Inyadullah, a

Northern Alliance troops enter Kabul in November 2001 to an enthusiastic welcome. The Taliban had left without a fight.

veteran fighter who had first gone to war in 1982, aged 16, to kill Soviet troops. Many Taliban fighters were prepared for a long war against the new Afghan government and its foreign allies. Some, however, became prisoners of the Northern Alliance. There were some surprise captives. John Walker Lindh was an American convert to Islam. He was identified after a battle in December 2001 inside Qala-i-Jhangi jail, when hundreds of Taliban prisoners fought their guards. Taken to the United States, Lindh was tried, and sentenced to 20 years in prison. Other detainees, suspected of

October 2001	▶ Hamid Karzai returns to Afghanistan from exile. He is the US choice as Afghanistan's new leader.
9–12 November 2001	▶ Northern Alliance forces capture Mazar-e Sharif.
14 November 2001	▶ The Northern Alliance takes Kabul.
25 November 2001	▶ CIA agent Johnny 'Mike' Spann is killed during the Qala-i-Jhangi prison battle at Mazar-e Sharif. He is the first US casualty in Afghanistan.
5 December 2001	▶ Northern Alliance leaders agree in Bonn, Germany, to form a provisional government, led by Hamid Karzai. Some leading Pashtun politicians are excluded from the talks.
22 December 2001	▶ British 'shoe bomber' Richard Reid is arrested on a flight to Miami, USA. Reid, an al-Qaeda convert, planned to blow up the plane with explosives hidden in his shoe. He is later given a life sentence.

Taliban prisoners peer out from cramped cells at Sheberghan Prison, near Mazar-e Sharif, in 2001.

terrorist links with al-Qaeda, were flown by the United States out of Afghanistan in a secret process known as extraordinary rendition. Their destination was Guantánamo Bay, in Cuba.

CROSS-REFERENCE
THE HUNT FOR
BIN LADEN:
PAGES 18–19
GUANTÁNAMO BAY:
PAGES 20–21

Foreign fighters

Many foreign fighters joined the Taliban in their fight against the Northern Alliance in Afghanistan. They included Pakistanis, Arabs, Yemenis and Chechens. Coalition interrogators who questioned captured foreign fighters said that some volunteers had been 'radicalized' – taught extreme views in support of a cause – in madrasas (Muslim religious schools). However, Muslim clerics in Pakistan and elsewhere insisted that the only function of the madrasas was to teach the Islamic faith.

The Hunt for Bin Laden

16 DECEMBER 2001

On 16 and 17 December 2001, in the bitter cold of winter, soldiers searched the White Mountains of eastern Afghanistan. They were looking for Osama bin Laden. In September, US Secretary of State Colin Powell had upped the reward for the capture of bin Laden to US$30 million. The Taliban insisted they did not know where bin Laden was, but intelligence reports suggested he might be in the Tora Bora caves. Close to the historic Khyber Pass, the caves were an old mujahideen hideout, used during the fighting against Soviet troops in the 1980s.

'MOST WANTED' GOES MISSING

US, British and German special forces followed the trail to Tora Bora, while drones fitted with cameras scanned the wild landscape for fugitives. Before a move on the caves was made, there were delays while Afghan commanders discussed a truce with al-Qaeda fighters. Then the attack began, with a bombing onslaught by warplanes including US B-52s. When the dust cleared, Tora Bora proved to be no more than a temporary hideout. Osama bin Laden had gone. He and his companions had probably crossed the mountains into Pakistan, perhaps while truce negotiations were in progress. The bombing of Tora Bora cost no coalition casualties, but the 'most wanted man in Afghanistan' had got away.

Osama bin Laden in one of his video appearances, in which he issued anti-American threats. At this time, October 2001, he was probably still in Afghanistan.

Al-Qaeda casualties

'There were arms and legs in the trees and the sides of the mountains were collapsing with the impact of the bombing.' Abu Jaffer, a Saudi supporter of Osama bin Laden, saw the air assault on Tora Bora, which caused heavy casualties among al-Qaeda fighters – about 200 were killed. Afghan forces attacking Tora Bora also suffered casualties (how many was not revealed) but no coalition soldiers were killed.

TIMELINE

HUNTING BIN LADEN AND A NEW GOVERNMENT 2001–2002

17 December 2001 ▶ The last cave at Tora Bora is searched; US troops continue searching into January 2002, but find no trace of Osama bin Laden.

22 December 2001 ▶ Hamid Karzai becomes chairman of Afghanistan's interim government.

January 2002 ▶ International peacekeeping troops of ISAF begin arriving in Afghanistan.

CONSOLIDATION AND INTERROGATION

In October 2001 Afghan leaders met in Bonn, Germany, and agreed to form a provisional government led by Hamid Karzai. Following this meeting, the United Nations Security Council authorized an International Security Assistance Force (ISAF) to act as a peacekeeper in Afghanistan. By the end of 2001, the coalition was confident the war was won, and that the new Afghan government and a retrained Afghan national army would take over security, while ISAF concentrated on aid and reconstruction. Refugees began to return home. UN peacekeeping troops from many nations flew in, along with planeloads of stores and equipment. The foreign soldiers built camps, went out on patrols and tried to make friends with the local people. Most hoped to be back home soon.

Afghan fighters watch smoke and dust rise from the Tora Bora caves. US bombers pounded the hideout before troops moved in, hoping to find Osama bin Laden.

CROSS-REFERENCE
NEW LEADERSHIP: PAGES 22–23
BIN LADEN'S LATER ACTIVITIES: PAGES 36–37

Guantánamo Bay

11 JANUARY 2002

On 11 January 2002, the first 20 terror suspects arrived at the US base at Guantánamo Bay on the island of Cuba. Because of the way prisoners were treated and interrogated, but not put on trial in proper courts, Guantánamo quickly became the focus of international criticism.

AGAINST THE RULES?

The US government maintained that the captives in Guantánamo were 'battlefield detainees', not prisoners of war (POWs). According to the United States, this distinction disqualified the captives from the rights and protection given by the Geneva conventions – the rules that protect all POWs. US Vice President Dick Cheney called the detainees 'very dangerous'. But as reports of the treatment of detainees began to leak out, many people around the world denounced the actions of the United States in Guantánamo as illegal and inhumane. Stories of torture such as 'water boarding' (pouring water over a prisoner's face to make him feel as if he is drowning) shocked most people. Guantánamo also stoked up anti-American feeling in Afghanistan. In May 2005, students protested in Kabul after reports of the alleged desecration of a Koran in Guantánamo. More than 14 people were reported to have been killed in this demonstration.

INSIDE GUANTÁNAMO

Pictures taken in Guantánamo Bay showed detainees wearing orange tops and bottoms, their legs chained, in open-air cages. To counter the allegations of humiliation and abuse, the US authorities insisted that the detainees were well-treated, that every Muslim was properly fed, and given a prayer mat and a copy of the Koran. In June 2006, the US Supreme Court ruled that the military commissions set up by the US government to try detainees were illegal. Nevertheless, detainees could still be held in Guantánamo indefinitely, without any trial.

There were some big names among the captives. Khalid Sheikh Mohammed, said to be number three in the al-Qaeda leadership, was captured in

US military police escort a Guantánamo Bay detainee to interrogation. Concerns about the procedures at Guantánamo were voiced by many in the United States, and around the world.

GUANTÁNAMO DETAINEES 2002–2009

11 January 2002	▶ The first 20 detainees arrive at Camp X-Ray, Guantánamo Bay. By March, the camp holds 300 detainees from over 33 countries.
29 April 2002	▶ Camp X-Ray is closed, and a larger 'facility', Camp Delta, is opened.
1 March 2003	▶ Khalid Sheikh Mohammed is captured in Pakistan.
16 January 2004	▶ Scandal about the abuse of Iraqi prisoners at Abu Ghraib prison, Baghdad, Iraq, adds to concern about Guantánamo.
15 March 2007	▶ Khalid Sheikh Mohammed admits planning the 9/11 attacks.
27 March 2007	▶ Australian David Hicks pleads guilty at Guantánamo to aiding terrorism. Hicks is the first detainee to face legal charges.
31 March 2008	▶ Ahmed Khalfan Ghailani, a Tanzanian captured in Pakistan in 2004, is charged with plotting the 1998 US embassy bombings.
March 2009	▶ President Obama announces that Guantánamo Bay is to shut down by 2010, though military tribunals will continue.

One detainee's story

Binyam Mohammed was born in Ethiopia in 1978. He told US interrogators that he was 'radicalized' while living in Britain. In June 2001 he went to Afghanistan, and in April 2002 he was arrested in Pakistan. The Americans flew him to Morocco, back to Afghanistan, and in September 2004 to Guantánamo Bay, where Mohammed confessed to attending al-Qaeda training camps. He later said that this confession was made under torture. He was released from Guantánamo in 2009.

Pakistan in 2003. But the reasons for other detainees to be held in Guantánamo were often less clear. Prisoners were questioned, but until 2007 there were no proper trials. Some detainees were released; others were held indefinitely because the US government said they could not be sent back to their home countries for fear of ill-treatment. In 2009, with fewer than 250 detainees left in custody, US President Barack Obama ordered Guantánamo Bay to be closed.

CROSS-REFERENCE **EXTRAORDINARY RENDITION:** PAGES 16–17

Orange-suited and masked, protesters in Australia demonstrate in 2008 to mark the sixth anniversary of the opening of Guantánamo Bay.

21

New Leadership

Refugees at a camp in Afghanistan. Many thousands of Afghan families were displaced by the fighting, and getting aid to refugees was often difficult and dangerous. Many refugees moved across the border into Pakistan.

On 13 June 2002, Hamid Karzai was chosen by the elders of Afghanistan's Loya Jirga (Grand Council) to be the next president of Afghanistan. Karzai had gone into exile during the Taliban years, returning to join the Northern Alliance in the war. Afghanistan's national assembly was reopened by Zahir Shah, also back from exile.

PROBLEMS AND HOPES

Taliban rule had left Afghanistan, a poor country slightly smaller than the US state of Texas, in a terrible state. In 2000 only seven per cent of pupils in school were girls, and the literacy rate was one of the world's lowest (below 30 per cent). One in six children died before the age of five. At least three million people were refugees. There were major environmental problems, too – not enough clean drinking water, overgrazing by livestock, and deforestation (people cut down trees for building and fuel). Average life expectancy was only 44 years.

The coalition promised aid, security and reconstruction. ISAF troops set about training the Afghan national army and police. President Bush talked of keeping the peace and rebuilding the Afghan economy. Most Afghans wanted to be left alone. Mohammed Asaf, an Afghan villager, summed up people's hopes. He told British journalists, '… all we want is progress and peace and democracy under the law of Islam'.

FALSE DAWN

By the summer of 2002, however, it was clear that the war was far from over. Taliban fighters, now known as insurgents, were regrouping in small mobile units to raid truck convoys and police stations. They were using the mountains and remote villages as

TIMELINE

NEW GOVERNMENT AND RECONSTRUCTION 2002

2 March 2002 ▶ US and Afghan forces attack al-Qaeda and Taliban forces in the Shahi-Kot mountains. Many fighters escape into Waziristan, Pakistan.

17 April 2002 ▶ Zahir Shah returns to Afghanistan from exile, although no longer king.

13 June 2002 ▶ Hamid Karzai becomes interim president of Afghanistan. He speaks optimistically of attracting foreign investment to rebuild his country.

1 July 2002 ▶ 48 civilian casualties are reported after a US plane fires on an Afghan wedding party.

4 July 2002 ▶ First British troops return to the UK after combat duty in Afghanistan.

their bases, making it difficult to isolate and attack them. The coalition relied on air power, but air strikes too often caused civilian casualties. On 1 July, a US plane dropped bombs that killed 48 Afghans at a wedding party in Uruzgan province. The Americans claimed that the party was being used as cover by the Taliban, who fired shots at the aircraft. However, firing guns into the air to celebrate a wedding is a tradition amongst many Afghans, and locals claimed that the shooting was entirely innocent. Such incidents soured relations between the Afghan population and the UN troops.

CROSS-REFERENCE ELECTIONS AND TERROR ATTACKS: PAGES 28–29 CIVILIANS UNDER ATTACK: PAGES 42–43

Perched on the ramp at the back of his helicopter, a CH-47 Chinook gunner scans the rugged Afghan hills.

Afghanistan from the air

Aid workers and the military in Afghanistan relied heavily on air transport. In 2001, Prue Peart, a British doctor, described how things looked from above: 'Flying over Afghanistan there is no sign of habitation and, with the rain failures, it looks the same shade of brown everywhere. The sun is warm, but it is the wind that makes it feel bitterly cold if you are not in a sheltered place ...'
Report in *The Guardian* newspaper, 14 February 2001.

Assassination Target

5 SEPTEMBER 2002

On 5 September 2002, President Karzai narrowly escaped assassination while visiting Kandahar for a family wedding. A gunman opened fire on his car, but he was unhurt. The gunman was shot dead by the president's bodyguards. It was not the first attempt on Karzai's life, nor would it be the last. He brushed aside the incident, saying, 'I'm fine, I expect things like this to happen.'

POLITICAL ASSASSINATIONS

Political assassinations had become part of Afghan life. Of several killings around this time, one of the most damaging was in July 2002, when an assassin in Kabul shot the Afghan vice president, Haji Abdul Qadir. Governor of Nangarhar province, Qadir was a Pashtun who had fought the Taliban, and one of the few ethnic Pashtuns in the new government. Like all politicians in Afghanistan, Qadir had made enemies, some of whom accused him of being a CIA agent with connections to the drugs underworld. His supporters, on the other hand, claimed that he had thrown his weight behind a crackdown on drug production. The cultivation of poppies for heroin was a major factor in Afghanistan's politics. The Taliban had tried to stamp out the drugs trade by stopping farmers growing poppies. But by 2002 the drugs trade was booming again. The Afghan government accused Taliban fighters of extorting 'protection' money from poppy farmers and using it to finance the war against the coalition.

'FRIENDLY FIRE'

ISAF troops faced growing dangers from Taliban ambushes, and at times from 'friendly fire' – getting shot at by their own side. On 17 April 2002, four Canadian soldiers on a training exercise were killed by two US F-16 jets. The pilots of the jets saw gunfire, thought the Canadians were members of the Taliban, and bombed them. It was a tragic reminder of the importance of good communications between ground and air, and between troops of different nations.

German soldiers of the ISAF stand guard around the vehicle of the assassinated Afghan vice president, Haji Abdul Qadir, in July 2002.

17 April 2002 ▶ Four Canadian soldiers are killed after being mistakenly bombed by US pilots.

6 July 2002 ▶ Haji Abdul Qadir, one of three Afghan vice presidents, is murdered.

5 September 2002 ▶ President Karzai narrowly escapes being shot dead in Kandahar.

21 October 2006 ▶ The Afghan government seizes 16 tonnes of drugs after targeting smugglers.

22 March 2009 ▶ The US envoy to Afghanistan, Richard Holbrooke, says anti-drugs efforts in Afghanistan have failed, despite years of effort and great cost.

Afghan farmers inspect flower heads in their poppy fields. Many villagers in rural areas of Afghanistan continue to rely on poppy-growing. No other crop offers such a profit.

CROSS-REFERENCE
TALIBAN
INSURGENTS:
PAGES 22–23

The poppy problem

The juice obtained from poppy seed heads can be processed to make opium, an important medical drug. It can also be used to make heroin, a dangerous narcotic that is traded by criminal gangs. When the Taliban banned poppy-growing it had the effect of pushing up the price of heroin, making the illegal trade even more profitable. Production restarted after the fall of the Taliban in 2001, and soon 90 per cent of the world's heroin was coming from Afghanistan's poppy fields. The coalition and the Afghan government tried to persuade farmers to grow other crops, such as citrus fruits, figs, dates and nuts. However, heroin offered such huge profits that one former Afghan government minister commented, 'if you got rid of drugs overnight the economy [in Afghanistan] would collapse'.

NATO Takes Command

On 11 August 2003, NATO took over command of ISAF. Until then, the international force had been under UN authority with ISAF command rotating between different countries. US troops were still the largest foreign contingent in Afghanistan, but after March 2003 the United States had a new battleground. After accusing Iraq's leader, Saddam Hussein, of possessing weapons of mass destruction (WMDs), the US and Britain launched a military attack on Iraq. Thousands of US troops headed for Iraq, and with the war against Saddam Hussein dominating the news, Afghanistan moved into a new era.

ISAF's ROLE

Afghanistan was NATO's first war outside Europe, although ISAF's role was, in theory, reconstruction rather than destruction. Some ISAF nations, such as the UK, had combat-ready troops in Afghanistan. Others, such as Japan, had committed only for non-combat tasks such as training, construction and distributing relief supplies. Some contingents were large (Britain had about 8,000 troops in Afghanistan); others small (Norway sent 500). ISAF commanders hoped their mission was peacekeeping, rather than fighting a resurgent Taliban. Their main concern was keeping law and order in a country full of weaponry, much of it in the hands of local militia groups and fighters loyal to tribal leaders. In 2003, for example, General Götz Gliemeroth of ISAF told Afghan militia leaders to remove heavy weapons (machine guns, grenade launchers and missiles) from Kabul.

MULTINATIONAL FORCE

By the end of 2003, ISAF had extended its operations beyond Kabul and it gradually assumed responsibility for security throughout Afghanistan. By 2009, ISAF had more than 50,000 soldiers from 44 countries – although the vast majority of troops were from the United States and Britain. Training and briefings only partly prepared these men and

Norwegian ISAF troops mount a roadblock on a street in Kabul. Norway was one of many countries to send a small contingent of soldiers to Afghanistan.

CROSS-REFERENCE
OPERATION
MOUNTAIN THRUST:
PAGES **32–33**
TROOP SURGE IN
IRAQ: PAGES **36–37**

TIMELINE	NATO IN AFGHANISTAN 2003–2009
August 2003	▶ NATO assumes command of ISAF's mission in Afghanistan.
December 2003	▶ NATO extends its ISAF mission beyond Kabul to an area formerly under German command, although Operation Enduring Freedom continues to be US-led.
October 2006	▶ NATO completes its ISAF expansion, taking over command of US-led forces in eastern Afghanistan.
2009	▶ ISAF forces total over 50,000; troops from all 26 NATO member-states have taken part in the Afghanistan operations.

women for the reality of life in Afghanistan. Many of the soldiers had little previous experience of combat, or of working together in a country few knew much about before stepping off the plane. Any soldier reading up on Afghanistan's history soon learned that foreign armies seldom had a comfortable stay.

Making progress?

NATO Secretary General Jaap de Hoop Scheffer said in 2009 that ISAF had to do more in Afghanistan. In particular, all countries must take their share of combat risks. But he was optimistic about progress in Afghanistan: 'Access to education is up tenfold. So is access to healthcare. And when I saw an Afghan pull out his Apple iPhone in Kabul... I saw another symbol of progress.'

A British soldier does his bit to 'win hearts and minds' by playing soccer with children in Kabul.

Elections and Terror Attacks

Workers in Kabul check ballot papers during the count for the presidential elections in 2004. The elections brought more women into Afghan politics.

On 9 October 2004, more than eight million people voted in Afghanistan's presidential elections. Hamid Karzai won 55 per cent of the vote. In 2005, elections were held for the national assembly and provincial councils. For the first time, the constitution required there to be at least two female delegates from each of the country's 34 provinces in the 249 elected representatives of the Wolesi Jirga (Lower House). A new Meshrano Jirga (Upper House) also met when the national assembly came together in December 2005.

IRAQ AND NATION-BUILDING

Afghanistan and Iraq had become twin problems for the United States. The Iraq War was soon over (2003) but the subsequent occupation of Iraq aroused widespread protests, especially among those Muslims who saw both wars as an attack on Islam. The US had many more troops in Iraq (over 100,000) than in Afghanistan, where it was keen to reduce its troop numbers to under 20,000 by 2006. President Bush spoke of 'nation-building'. He hoped Iraq and Afghanistan would become Western-style democracies – an ambitious goal, even if their peoples wanted it.

In Afghanistan, ISAF helped to rebuild schools, pipelines, irrigation ditches, wells and roads. The Afghan national army received training and equipment including guns, ammunition, uniforms, tanks and helicopters. New recruits were encouraged to join the Afghan national police. The 2004–05 elections raised hopes, despite a harsh winter that killed hundreds of villagers. Yet the Taliban had not been frozen out. They were still armed and dangerous, and planning how to overthrow the Karzai government.

TIMELINE

NEW HOPES AND TERROR ATTACKS ABROAD
2002–2005

12 October 2002 ▶ A nightclub bomb kills 202 people on the island of Bali, Indonesia.

11 March 2004 ▶ Terrorists explode bombs in four rush-hour trains in Madrid, Spain; 191 people die.

9 October 2004 ▶ Elections in Afghanistan; voters elect Hamid Karzai as president. He takes office on 7 December.

7 July 2005 ▶ 52 people are killed and 700 injured in bombings of Tube trains and a bus in London, UK.

18 September 2005 ▶ Afghans vote in elections for 34 provincial councils and the Wolesi Jirga (Lower House) of the national assembly, for the first time since 1969.

December 2005 ▶ Afghanistan's new national assembly meets.

TERROR LINKS

Intelligence suggested that al-Qaeda still had training camps and bases in Afghanistan, especially along the border with Pakistan. Terrorist attacks in Bali (2002), Madrid (2004) and London (2005) were all blamed on al-Qaeda, or extremist groups linked to al-Qaeda. Bin Laden approved of these worldwide activities. Speaking on the Arabic satellite television channel Al-Jazeera, he said the killing of tourists in Bali was a 'punishment' for the West.

Hamid Karzai (second left) was inaugurated as Afghanistan's president on 7 December 2004. Beside him at the ceremony was former king, Zahir Shah (left).

CROSS-REFERENCE
MURDER AND SUICIDE BOMBS: PAGES **36–37**
CIVILIANS UNDER ATTACK: PAGES **42–43**

London bombers

On 14 July 2005, suicide bombers in London killed 52 people. The four bombers lived in Britain, but had travelled to Pakistan, possibly for training. The deputy leader of al-Qaeda, Ayman al-Zawahri, claimed that the bombings were masterminded by al-Qaeda, although British investigations found no clear evidence of the group's involvement. In April 2009, British prime minister Gordon Brown told British troops in Afghanistan: 'There is a line of terror that goes from Afghanistan and the border area of Pakistan right back to the streets of our own countries … if we do not fight back against al-Qaeda and the Taliban, then people are less safe.'

Helicopter Down

On 28 June 2005, 16 US soldiers were killed when the Taliban shot down a Chinook helicopter that was on its way to rescue a four-man US special forces team from a battle in northeast Afghanistan. The Taliban claimed they brought down the Chinook with a rocket-propelled grenade.

HELICOPTERS AT WAR

In a country like Afghanistan, with few good roads and a rugged landscape, aircraft and especially helicopters play a key role in transporting soldiers and supplies. The big, twin-rotor CH-47 Chinook is the 'workhorse' helicopter; smaller, heavily armed 'gunships' such as the UH-60 Black Hawk support ground troops in combat.

All modern warplanes, including helicopters, are stuffed with secret electronics. When a Black Hawk was shot at by the Taliban in July 2008, the US pilots managed to crash-land the aircraft and get away. A second helicopter was quickly sent in to blow up the wreckage, before the Taliban could get at it and learn its secrets.

HAZARDS AND PROPAGANDA

Afghanistan's climate and terrain are tough on all machinery. Helicopters are complex aircraft, and an Afghan dust storm can be as dangerous as enemy missiles. On 6 April 2005, a US Chinook crashed during a dust storm in Ghazni; 18 Americans, three of them civilians, were killed. A helicopter down was always a propaganda boost for the Taliban. When an Afghan army helicopter crashed in January 2009, the government blamed bad weather; the Taliban, however, said they had shot it down. There were many 'wars of words' between the two sides, with the Taliban claiming to have destroyed many more aircraft and vehicles, and to have killed more Afghan and coalition troops, than were admitted by NATO and US commanders. At the start of the war, US aircraft flew out of

Helicopters are often the only way to ferry in supplies to remote camps. Soldiers in the mountains rely on Chinooks and other helicopters for food, water, fuel and ammunition.

CROSS-REFERENCE
AFGHANISTAN FROM
THE AIR: PAGES 22–23

TIMELINE

HELICOPTERS AT WAR
2005–2009

6 April 2005 ▶ A US Chinook comes down in a dust storm.

28 June 2005 ▶ A US Chinook crashes, killing 16 US soldiers; the Taliban claim they shot it down.

16 August 2005 ▶ 17 Spanish soldiers are killed when their helicopter crashes.

2 July 2008 ▶ A US Black Hawk helicopter is shot down by the Taliban.

15 January 2009 ▶ An Afghan MI-17 helicopter crashes; among the 13 dead is Fazel Ahmad Sayar, the Afghan general in command of western Afghanistan.

bases in states across the border from Afghanistan, but in July 2005 Uzbekistan asked the US to leave its airbases. Early in 2009 Kyrgyzstan did the same, saying the 'rent' was too low, but then changed its mind. The US was prepared to pay, to ease transportation and aircraft movements in and out of Afghanistan.

The long-serving Chinook

The Chinook helicopter has been around since the 1960s, and has seen combat in the Vietnam, Iraq and Afghanistan wars. It can carry troops into battle, evacuate the wounded, fly in food, fuel and ammunition, and even airlift a tank. The Chinook is fast for a big helicopter, with a top speed of just under 322 kph. However the heat and dust, and ice and snow of Afghanistan's deserts and mountains pose stern tests for both the Chinooks and their pilots.

Helicopters are vital for evacuating the wounded. This casualty was flown into Kandahar military hospital.

Operation Mountain Thrust

From 15 May 2006 and onwards into July, Afghan and NATO forces attacked the Taliban in southern Afghanistan. Operation Mountain Thrust was the biggest offensive since the war began in 2001, made necessary by the Taliban's growing threat to security in the south. The Taliban were particularly active in three provinces: Helmand (where British troops were based), Uruzgan (Dutch) and Kandahar (Canadian).

FIGHTING AGAIN

By 2006, there were more than 30,000 ISAF coalition troops in Afghanistan. Many had still not yet fired a shot on Afghan territory except in training, yet in the south of the country the Taliban were becoming increasingly disruptive, taking over towns, harassing road transport, killing government officials and teachers, and targeting schools to disrupt the government's education programme. Operation Mountain Thrust was intended to regain Afghan government and ISAF control of southern Afghanistan.

RESTORING CONTROL

The conventional military thinking was that the Taliban must be beaten in battle. However, some Afghan leaders and ISAF commanders thought that negotiation might bring local

settlements with the Taliban. However, talks between village elders, government officials and coalition soldiers seldom achieved much. By the time Mountain Thrust ended in July, the military claimed the deaths of more than 1,000 Taliban at a cost of 155 coalition casualties. On 1 August 2006, responsibility for ISAF security operations in southern Afghanistan passed to NATO from the US-led coalition. NATO forces (British, Canadian and Dutch), supported

Artillery forms part of NATO's weaponry to blast Taliban strongholds. These gunners were taking part in Operation Mountain Thrust, 10 July 2006.

Even though their classroom is a tent, these girl students in Kabul are fortunate their education has resumed. The Taliban have attacked many schools.

TIMELINE

REGAINING CONTROL IN THE SOUTH 2006

29 March 2006 ▶ Taliban fighters attack the Afghan national army and coalition troops at Lashgar base.

29 May 2006 ▶ In Kabul, a US truck crashes into a crowd, killing three people. In the ensuing riot, 14 more civilians die.

31 July 2006 ▶ Operation Mountain Thrust ends. Next day (1 August 2006) NATO takes over responsibility for peacekeeping in southern Afghanistan.

August 2006 ▶ The UN says Taliban attacks on schools mean 100,000 Afghan children are missing out on their education.

5 September 2006 ▶ The Pakistan government signs an agreement with pro-Taliban militants in the border region of Waziristan to end fighting there.

November 2006 ▶ US Defense Secretary Donald Rumsfeld resigns after criticism of US policy in Iraq and Afghanistan. His replacement is Robert Gates.

by the Afghan national army, immediately became involved in heavy fighting. In October 2006, 12,000 US troops were switched to NATO command to carry out counter-insurgency operations in eastern Afghanistan. While training and reconstruction were still going on, the renewed war against the Taliban was hotting up.

CROSS-REFERENCE BATTLES FOR HELMAND: PAGES 34–35

Hopes to end the insurgency

The Governor of Zabul province, Dilbar Jan Arman, told *The Guardian* newspaper (15 June 2006) that Afghan leaders and US commanders were working closely together in Operation Mountain Thrust. He said, 'We will search for the Taliban, wherever they are. We seek to disrupt their underground networks. We hope it will be a success.' Despite such hopes, many Afghans still resented the presence of foreign troops.

Operation Achilles

A British soldier amid the debris of war in Musa Qala, Helmand province, in December 2007.

On 6 March 2007 NATO launched another offensive, code-named Operation Achilles, in British-patrolled Helmand province. Helmand is roughly half the size of England and it is mainly desert, freezing cold (−15°C) in winter and scorching hot (45°C) in summer.

TALIBAN TACTICS

Coalition strategy was to drive the Taliban from key sites such as the Kajakai hydroelectric dam (long disused), fight them out of ancient mud-walled forts, and return Taliban-infiltrated towns to local people. However, it was not Taliban strategy to risk losing many men for one town. Mullah Dadullah, a top Taliban commander, told journalists; 'Taking cities is not our present tactic… We have attacked and occupied certain locations for a short period … but we will always retreat to our safe bases.' One example of this tactic was the town of Musa Qala in Helmand, which

changed hands several times during 2006–07. In December 2007 coalition soldiers finally retook the town. Corporal Danny Groves of the British army's Royal Irish Regiment wrote in his diary about the problems of keeping such gains under enemy fire. He imagined the town as a dartboard; 'All we had was a 100 m by 100 m square dartboard at which [the Taliban] threw darts in the form of RPGs [rocket-propelled grenades] whenever they fancied.'

BOMBS AND HOSTAGES

On 27 February 2007, the Taliban bombed Bagram airbase during a visit by US Vice President Dick Cheney. Foreign aid workers and journalists also came under attack. In March 2007, an Italian reporter called Daniele Mastrogiacomo was kidnapped. His driver and an Afghan journalist were killed, but the reporter was freed after the Italian government asked President

TIMELINE	BATTLES, TALKS AND HOSTAGES 2007
12 May 2007	▶ Mullah Dadullah, the Taliban commander in south Afghanistan, is killed by coalition forces.
30 May 2007	▶ Operation Achilles ends.
30 July 2007	▶ The last South Korean hostages are released.
September 2007	▶ A Canadian opinion poll reports that one in three Afghan civilians think the Taliban will return as soon as foreign troops leave. Eighty-five per cent think the government must talk to the Taliban.
11 December 2007	▶ Battle of Musa Qala ends; coalition troops retake the town.

Life on patrol

On patrol, NATO troops usually travelled in all-terrain vehicles, keeping their eyes open for the Toyota Hilux trucks often used by Taliban fighters among the brightly painted 'jingly' trucks of civilians – so-called because of the jingling chains hanging from them. Fresh water was scarce, so each soldier carried at least three litres of water. At night, the soldiers ate 'boil in the bag' rations and looked forward to proper meals back in camp. Canadian soldier Brian Sanders wrote in his blog: 'there is nothing, and I mean absolutely nothing, in this world that boosts morale better than a fresh meal. Anything that can make a ration not taste like a ration is welcomed.'

Karzai to free five Taliban prisoners. On 19 July 2007, the Taliban seized 23 South Korean Christian missionaries. They killed two, but released the remaining 21 in exchange for cash and South Korea's withdrawal from the coalition. By August 2007, President Karzai admitted the situation had deteriorated, and in September he said he was willing to meet for talks with the Taliban leader, Mullah Omar.

CROSS-REFERENCE NATO IN AFGHANISTAN: PAGES 26–27

Freed hostage Daniele Mastrogiacomo waves as he arrives home in Italy.

Murder and Suicide Bombs

On 17 February 2008, a suicide bomber killed 100 people in Kandahar. Suicide attacks had been rare in Afghanistan, so this and other similar attacks were evidence of changing Taliban tactics. The United Nations stated that Afghanistan was experiencing its worst year of violence since 2001, with more than 5,000 deaths caused by Taliban activity. A British organization, the International Council on Security and Development, estimated that the Taliban were active across 70 per cent of Afghanistan by the end of 2008.

FOREIGN CONNECTIONS

In fact, 2007 had ended with some optimism. In Iraq, a US 'troop surge' (sending in thousands of extra troops to fight insurgents) had improved security, allowing US commander General David Petraeus to recommend troop withdrawals. Optimists hoped that Afghanistan would follow the same route. The main obstacles to peace in Afghanistan were, in US eyes at least, Iran and Pakistan. The United States accused Iran of supplying weapons and explosives to the Taliban, a charge rejected in August 2007 by Iran's president, Mahmoud Ahmadinejad. Pakistan remained a source of support for both the Taliban and al-Qaeda – President Karzai described Afghanistan and Pakistan as

'conjoined twins'. In August 2007, Pakistan's President Musharraf said, 'There is no doubt Afghan militants are supported from Pakistan soil'. In October 2007 Pakistani and Taliban forces clashed in Pakistan's Waziristan province. In December, Benazir Bhutto, Pakistan's former prime minister, was assassinated in Rawalpindi, Pakistan. Her murder was linked to al-Qaeda.

BIN LADEN'S LAST TAPE?

Al-Qaeda leader Osama bin Laden continued to issue taped messages, often linking the war in Afghanistan with the conflicts in Iraq and in the Middle East between Israel and Palestine. In September 2008, in a video to mark the sixth anniversary of 9/11, he warned the United States that it was still vulnerable to attack. Yet

This March 2008 suicide attack on a Canadian army convoy in Kandahar killed an Afghan civilian and wounded others.

TIMELINE

MURDER AND MEDIA STORIES 2008–2009

28 February 2008 ▶ Prince Harry's British army posting in Afghanistan is cut short after news of his being there leaks to the media.

27 April 2008 ▶ President Karzai escapes another assassination attempt.

7 November 2008 ▶ A Taliban suicide attack kills six Afghan members of parliament and 53 other people in the town of Baghlan.

November 2008 ▶ Osama bin Laden tells Europeans to break with the United States, and stop fighting the Taliban.

March 2009 ▶ The US government offers US$11 million bounty for the seizure of three al-Qaeda leaders suspected of planning Benazir Bhutto's murder.

Backed by the United States, Benazir Bhutto seemed a likely leader of Pakistan after her return from exile in 2007. Shortly after attending this rally in Rawalpindi, she was killed by a suicide bomb, on 27 December 2007. Her husband, Asif Ali Zardari, was elected as president in September 2008.

mystery continued to surround bin Laden's whereabouts. His health was reportedly poor, and in 2009 Pakistani officials suggested that he might be dead. Nevertheless the search for bin Laden continued. In June 2009 the CIA chief Leon Panetta told the press that the CIA thought bin Laden was probably in Pakistan, and might be 'flushed out' by Pakistan army operations there.

CROSS-REFERENCE
CROSS-BORDER RAIDS: **PAGES 40–41**
MURDERS OF HUMAN RIGHTS ACTIVISTS: **PAGES 42–43**

Remember Afghanistan's history

Although Afghanistan's leaders publicly supported the coalition's efforts, they insisted the world recognize that Afghanistan had a proud history of independence. On a visit to the United States in 2007, Afghanistan's defence minister and former mujahideen fighter, Abdul Rahim Wardak, told his hosts: 'This is our country and we have died for it for thousands of years. Throughout history, our only pride was that we defended our country.'

Cross-Border Raids

10 JUNE 2008

On 10 June 2008, a US air strike into Pakistan killed 11 Pakistani soldiers. The mountain valleys of the border country between Afghanistan and Pakistan had become a new battleground. The Taliban and al-Qaeda had attracted support from militants, and turned the border region into a stronghold. On 15 June, President Karzai said the Afghan army would pursue Taliban militants across the border into Pakistan when necessary.

BORDER TENSIONS

The Pakistan army tried to persuade Pashtun tribal leaders in Pakistan to help fight the militants, but with limited success. In August 2007, militants captured more than 200 Pakistani soldiers and held them hostage for the release of Taliban prisoners. In 2008, however, the Pakistan army claimed to have killed 1,500 militants in escalating border clashes. Unfortunately, these fights also brought US and Pakistani troops into conflict, as US troops went after retreating Taliban, firing missiles across the border at suspected hideouts.

In September 2008, US troops exchanged fire with Pakistani soldiers during one such incursion. Pakistan protested, saying that these actions only increased the anti-US feeling in Pakistan. In response, the US commander, General McKiernan, repeated the widely held charge that Pakistani intelligence (ISI) knew more about Taliban activities than it was saying. The United States feared the 'destabilization' of Pakistan, particularly as it has nuclear weapons.

Protesters in Pakistan make their views known. US air strikes and cross-border raids increased anti-American feeling even as Pakistan stepped up its military activities against the Taliban.

TIMELINE	TENSION IN PAKISTAN 2007–2008

3 November 2007 ▶ General Musharraf declares a state of emergency in Pakistan, saying judges and lawyers are undermining his fight against terrorism. There are widespread protests.

28 November 2007 ▶ Musharraf steps down as army chief, and next day is sworn in for a new term as Pakistan's president.

27 December 2007 ▶ Pakistani political leader Benazir Bhutto is shot by a gunman, who blows himself up.

18 August 2008 ▶ Musharraf resigns as president of Pakistan.

September 2008 ▶ American and Pakistani troops clash in the Afghan border region after US special forces enter Pakistan.

23 November 2008 ▶ Pakistan's foreign minister, Shah Mahmood Qureshi, says the ISI is no longer 'politically active'. The ISI had been accused of helping the Taliban.

WINNING OR NOT?

'We are still a nation deep in pain and misery,' commented President Karzai in October 2008. He called on the coalition to change its tactics; the Afghan people were suffering too much for little real gain. Afghanistan needed more soldiers, more helicopters and more roads. It needed security so that farmers could travel to market safely, and villagers could run their affairs without fear of the Taliban turning up the next day to punish them for helping the coalition. Military commanders tried to sound realistic yet optimistic. Admiral Michael Mullen, chairman of the US Joint Chiefs of Staff, told a US Congressional hearing on 10 September 2008, 'I'm not convinced we're winning it in Afghanistan. I am convinced we can.'

President Karzai (left) addresses a press conference with President Musharraf of Pakistan.

CROSS-REFERENCE AF-PAK: PAGES 40–41

Crisis in Pakistan

On 18 August 2008, General Musharraf resigned as Pakistan's president. At times a reluctant ally of President Bush, he had been Pakistan's 'strongman' since the army seized power in 1999, but stepped down as army chief in November 2007. Threatened with charges of corruption, by 2008 he had lost support, and quit. Musharaff was succeeded by Asif Ali Zardari, leader of the Pakistan People's Party since the assassination in December 2007 of his wife, Benazir Bhutto.

Prison Break and Tensions

On 13 June 2008, Taliban fighters made a daring attack on Sarposa Prison in Kandahar. Up to 1,000 prisoners, including 300 Taliban suspects, escaped. It was a serious blow to the Afghan security forces. Kandahar is one of the country's major cities, the prison was supposedly well guarded, and the escape was a massive propaganda success for the Taliban.

ESCAPE FROM SARPOSA

In May 2008, prisoners in Sarposa had gone on hunger strike. Some claimed that they had been in jail for two years without trial. When the government agreed to review their cases, the strike ended. At about 9 pm on 13 June, a tanker truck driven by a Taliban suicide bomber crashed into the prison. The explosion blasted a hole in the wall through which prisoners ran away, while about 30 Taliban fighters on motorbikes fired rockets and grenades at the Afghan police. The attack went undetected, even though a nearby airbase was packed with surveillance systems.

INDIA AND PAKISTAN

On 7 July, a truck bomb attack on the Indian embassy in Kabul killed 54 people. This attack raised tensions between India and Pakistan, both countries with close links to Afghanistan. During the Taliban

regime in Afghanistan, which was backed by Pakistan, India had strongly supported the Northern Alliance. India and Pakistan also have their own disagreements, most notably over the disputed state of

After the prison break in Kandahar a vehicle lies overturned amid the wreckage caused by explosives and rocket fire.

Af-Pak

Pakistan is so closely linked with Afghanistan that the term Af-Pak has come into use to describe policy in the region. Both countries share a people (the Pashtuns), a long border and a religion (Islam). One of very few states to support the Afghan Taliban, Pakistan found itself in a difficult position after 9/11. It became a US ally in the 'war on terror' and sent thousands of troops to the country's border regions to hunt down Taliban and al-Qaeda members. But many people in Pakistan saw their government's alliance with the United States as a mistake, and there were frequent anti-US demonstrations.

TIMELINE	**MOUNTING COSTS 2008**

February 2008 ▶	The US defence budget (US$515 billion) is the biggest since World War II.
2 June 2008 ▶	A suicide bomber attacks the Danish embassy in Islamabad, the capital of Pakistan. Al-Qaeda in Afghanistan says the bombing is punishment for the publication in Denmark of alleged anti-Muslim cartoons.
12 June 2008 ▶	At a meeting in Paris, more than 80 nations and aid agencies pledge US$21 billion in aid to Afghanistan. Drought and crop failure in Afghanistan mean eight million people are going hungry.
13 June 2008 ▶	The Sarposa Prison escape is a blow to Afghan security.
13 July 2008 ▶	The Taliban attack the NATO base at Wanat, killing nine US soldiers.
19 August 2008 ▶	Ten French soldiers are killed in a Taliban ambush in the Uzbin Valley – the worst single incident of casualties suffered by France in Afghanistan.

Kashmir. So after the Indian embassy bombing, when Pakistan claimed that the terrorists responsible for the attack were either al-Qaeda or Taliban, India responded by accusing Pakistan's security agency, the Inter-Services Intelligence (ISI), of aiding the terrorists. This charge was strongly denied by Pakistan.

DIPLOMATIC AND MILITARY STRESSES

With coalition military casualties mounting, public opinion in the United States and Europe began to shift against the war. The US Department of Defense reported a steep increase in the number of soldiers with stress disorders, and in 2007, 115 US soldiers committed suicide, an unusually high total. Veterans claimed that fighting wars in both Iraq and Afghanistan imposed intolerable strains on individual soldiers, as well as on the army's resources.

US military personnel salute a flag-draped coffin. The bodies of US and NATO troops killed in Afghanistan are usually flown home.

CROSS-REFERENCE BORDER TENSIONS: PAGES 38–39

Civilians Under Attack

22 AUGUST 2008

Villagers pick through the rubble of their homes after a US air strike. Bombs and rockets kill innocent civilians, as well as their intended targets.

On 22 August 2008, a US-led air strike in west Afghanistan killed a number of civilians. The Afghan government and the UN estimated the number of dead to be 90; US sources said about 33. The UN reported that more than 2,000 Afghan civilians had been killed in 2008, 55 per cent of this number by insurgents – the rest by Afghan army or ISAF operations, and mostly by air strikes. President Karzai asked the UN to tell ISAF to end 'bombardments, house searching and unnecessary detentions of Afghans by international forces'.

CIVILIAN CASUALTIES

The Afghan government blamed the coalition for targeting villages. The coalition responded by saying that the Taliban used villages as hideouts.

NATO had insufficient troops on the ground, and often called in air strikes, increasing the risk of civilian casualties. Coalition dead in 2008 totalled 294, the highest death toll since the war began in 2001. Taliban hit squads also targeted human rights activists, murdering them in the street.

WOMEN AND CHILDREN KILLED

In May 2009, US jets bombed two villages at Bala Baluk in Farah province, west Afghanistan. Bala Baluk is a Pashtun region, where the Taliban are reported to have a strong foothold. According to the Afghan government 95 of the 130 to 140 dead were under the age of 18. The International Red Cross reported 'There were women and children who were killed. It seemed

| TIMELINE | CIVILIAN DEATHS 2008 |

September 2008	▶ The New York City-based Human Rights Watch reports that civilian deaths from coalition air strikes in Afghanistan almost tripled from 2006 to 2007.
14 October 2008	▶ The Afghan government claims fighters from Iraq are joining the Taliban.
3 November 2008	▶ A US air attack on a wedding party kills 26 militants and 37 civilians, according to Afghan sources. US officials claim that 20 civilians died.
25 November 2008	▶ President Karzai appeals to the UN Security Council to end civilian casualties. He is reported as inviting Taliban leader Mullah Omar to negotiate; the Taliban refuse.

The killing of Sitara Achakzai horrified many people. Demonstrators in Kandahar came out to display her picture and pay tribute to her courage in defying the Taliban.

Gunned down

Sitara Achakzai, a campaigner for women's rights, was a member of the provincial council in Kandahar. Forced into exile in Germany in the 1990s by Taliban rule, on her return home she encouraged Afghan women to enter public life. This made her a target. After surviving a suicide bomb attack in Kandahar in April 2009, she bought tickets to fly to Canada. Two weeks later she was shot dead by Taliban gunmen.

they were trying to shelter in houses…' A human rights group, the Afghanistan Rights Monitor, accused the Taliban of using civilians as human shields, but said the US response was 'excessive'. The US regional commander General David Petraeus ordered an investigation. In such cases, compensation was usually offered – US$1,000 for each dead civilian.

CROSS-REFERENCE
OPERATION
ENDURING
FREEDOM: PAGES
14–15

An Exit Strategy?

In a television interview on 23 March 2009, the new US president, Barack Obama, admitted that the problem of Afghanistan was 'more difficult than Iraq' and that the United States needed an 'exit strategy'. The President spoke of increasing humanitarian aid, more training for the Afghan army, and more help for Pakistan in its fight against insurgents. He said that the Afghan national army would grow from 70,000 to over 130,000, and he asked the European nations to increase their forces in Afghanistan.

A NEW DIRECTION?

In May 2009, US Lieutenant-General Stanley McChrystal took over from General David McKiernan, ISAF commander since only June 2008. This was a hint of new strategies to come, as well as an indication of US concern that it was not winning its longest war since Vietnam. Some NATO planners thought a decisive military victory was unlikely, and the Afghan government made new approaches to the Taliban, suggesting talks. The response was not encouraging. The Taliban leader, Mullah Omar, said he would talk only when foreign troops had left. Meanwhile, the United States was spending more on defence since World War II while, like the rest of the world, facing severe economic problems after the worst financial collapse (2008) since the Great Depression of the 1930s.

In May 2009, President Obama meets the new US commander in Afghanistan, Lieutenant-General Stanley McChrystal.

Public views

After the replacement of General McKiernan in 2009, US Defense Secretary Robert Gates said it was time for 'fresh thinking'. In March 2009, a US presidential aide, Richard Holbrooke, agreed that the answer was not just more soldiers and bombs: 'What we can't do is think that just a military approach in Afghanistan is going to be able to solve our problems'.

TIMELINE	**NEW BEGINNINGS, OLD PROBLEMS 2008–2009**
September 2008	▶ Afghan and Taliban representatives meet for talks in Saudi Arabia. In October, Afghan and Pakistani tribal leaders agree to contact the Taliban to explore the possibility of a settlement.
January 2009	▶ Barack Obama takes office as president of the United States. He promises more aid to Afghanistan and announces his intention to shut down Guantánamo Bay.
February 2009	▶ Kyrgyzstan asks the US to leave its airbases, used by US planes to fly into Afghanistan.
May 2009	▶ President Obama says that the 'Af-Pak' crisis is the focus of US foreign policy. General David McKiernan is replaced as US top soldier in Afghanistan by Lieutenant-General Stanley McChrystal, a counter-insurgency specialist.

NO END IN SIGHT

By 2009, Taliban militants in Pakistan controlled both the Swat Valley and the Buner district – which lies only 100 km from Pakistan's capital, Islamabad. US Secretary of State Hillary Clinton said Pakistan was 'abdicating to the Taliban' by allowing the militants to control the region. Thousands of refugees poured out of the Swat Valley in May 2009, as the Pakistan army prepared to launch a major offensive against the Taliban militants. Accounts of atrocities committed by the Taliban in areas of Pakistan under their control also caused a change in public mood in Pakistan.

In Afghanistan, the death toll has continued to mount: 4,500 Afghan soldiers, over 1,000 coalition soldiers and anything between 10,000 and 30,000 civilians since the war began. In June 2009 another surge of troops began a new initiative in southern Afghanistan to try to remove the Taliban. Meanwhile life for the majority of Afghans remained as hard and dangerous as ever. No end was yet in sight.

Refugees from the Swat Valley, Pakistan, where the Pakistan army launched a full-scale offensive against the Taliban in 2009.

CROSS-REFERENCE LIFE UNDER THE TALIBAN: PAGES 10–11

Key Figures in the War in Afghanistan

GEORGE W BUSH (1946–), PRESIDENT OF THE UNITED STATES

George Walker Bush became president of the United States in 2000. In 2001 the 9/11 terrorist attacks threw the country into crisis. Bush ordered the attack on Afghanistan against the Taliban and al-Qaeda, and in 2003 initiated the Iraq War against Saddam Hussein. The wars, and the controversy surrounding the Guantánamo Bay detention camp, slashed Bush's popularity at home, and increased anti-US feeling abroad. After two terms in office, Bush left the White House in 2009.

OSAMA BIN LADEN (1957–), LEADER OF AL-QAEDA

The leader of the conspiracy behind the 9/11 attacks on the United States, as well as other terrorist attacks, Osama bin Laden was born in Riyadh, Saudi Arabia, where his father ran a construction business. After university in Jeddah, he went to Afghanistan in the 1980s to fight with the mujahideen against the Soviets. He set up a base for Arab fighters in Pakistan. After founding al-Qaeda in 1988–89 he returned to Saudi Arabia, and was later active in both Sudan and Somalia. Intelligence experts believe that bin Laden was in Afghanistan when the war began, and that he moved to Pakistan to escape coalition forces.

HAMID KARZAI (1957–), PRESIDENT OF AFGHANISTAN

Born in Kandahar, Karzai was the hereditary chief of one of Afghanistan's foremost Pashtun clans, or extended families, the Populzai. He joined the resistance against the Soviets in the 1980s, and served in the Rabbani government until its overthrow in 1996. Rejecting a Taliban offer to be UN ambassador, Karzai left Afghanistan for exile. Karzai returned to Afghanistan in October 2001, and in June 2002 was named president of the interim government. In 2004, he became the first Afghan president to be elected by a popular majority vote.

AHMAD SHAH MASSOUD (1953–2001), NORTHERN ALLIANCE LEADER

A Tajik from northern Afghanistan, known to his followers as the 'Lion of Panjshir', Massoud was a mujahideen general who fought the communists in 1978–79, the Soviet invaders through the 1980s, and the Taliban in the 1990s. A skilful strategist, Massoud was a charismatic leader of the Northern Alliance. His assassination by the Taliban took place two days before the 9/11 attacks in 2001.

STANLEY MCCHRYSTAL (1954–), ISAF COMMANDER

Trained at West Point military academy, McChrystal rose through the US army to take charge of Joint Special Operations Command (JSOC), said to be the most secretive force in the US military. An expert in counter-insurgency and covert operations, General McChrystal is reputed to have masterminded the killing of the al-Qaeda leader in Iraq, Abu Musala al-Zarqawi. He was appointed to be America's top soldier in Afghanistan in 2009.

PERVEZ MUSHARRAF (1943–), PRESIDENT OF PAKISTAN

General Musharraf seized power in Pakistan in 1999, after ousting Prime Minister Nawaz Sharif in a military coup. He was president from 2001, when he agreed (contrary to earlier Pakistani support for the Taliban) to back the United States in the war against the Taliban in Afghanistan. The relationship between Pakistan and the United States later came under strain when US forces pursued militants into Pakistan. Musharraf stepped down as president in 2008, and Pakistan returned to civilian government.

BARACK OBAMA (1961–), PRESIDENT OF THE UNITED STATES

The first African-American president of the United States, Obama was a lawyer by training and entered the US Senate in 2004. Promising 'a new kind of politics', he convincingly won the 2008 presidential election, defeating his Republican rival John McCain. On taking office in 2009, Obama and new secretary of state Hillary Clinton promised new initiatives in foreign policy. Obama promised the closure of Guantánamo Bay, and a rundown of US troops in Iraq, but announced an increase in the US military commitment to Afghanistan.

MOHAMMED OMAR (1959?–), LEADER OF THE TALIBAN

A Pashtun, known to his followers as 'commander of the faithful', Mullah Omar (a mullah is a Muslim teacher or scholar) fought against the communist government and the Soviets in Afghanistan in the 1980s. He met Osama bin Laden and in 1992–93 formed the Taliban, a group that wished to impose strict Islamic government on Afghanistan. After the Taliban's removal by the Northern Alliance and coalition in 2001, Omar went into hiding. It is believed that he continues to direct Taliban policy.

BURHANUDDIN RABBANI (1940–), AFGHAN POLITICIAN

Born in northern Afghanistan, Rabbani was leader of Jamiat-e Islami Afghanistan (the Islamic Society of Afghanistan), and a leading figure in the Northern Alliance. An Islamic scholar and academic, he helped lead resistance to the communist regime and Soviets, and served as Afghanistan's president 1992–96. Forced from office by the Taliban in September 1996, he was reinstated in November 2001 as interim president, before handing over to President Karzai.

Glossary

al-Qaeda   terrorist group founded by Osama bin Laden to promote the Wahhabi (Saudi) brand of Islamic fundamentalism

burka   garment worn by a Muslim woman that covers her from head to foot

Central Intelligence Agency (CIA)   intelligence-gathering organization of the United States

coalition   group of nations united by a common aim

Cold War   period of hostility (1940s–1990s) between communist and non-communist blocs, particularly between the Soviet Union and the United States

communism   system of government based on the ideas of the 19th-century German philosopher Karl Marx, characterized by state control

cruise missile   guided missile launched from a ship or submarine, able to locate and destroy targets with precision

ethnic group   a group of people united by language, customs and tradition

extraordinary rendition   secret process for moving suspects between countries for questioning, used by the United States

guerrilla   soldier who is not part of a regular army, often fighting a resistance war against an occupying force or invader

Hazara   tribal group in central Afghanistan, who speak a Persian dialect

heroin   narcotic drug, made from the opium poppy

insurgent   a rebel; used to describe militants fighting a government

International Security Assistance Force (ISAF)   international force authorized by the United Nations to restore peace in Afghanistan

jihad   means 'struggle' in Arabic; a holy war believed by Muslims to be at God's command

Koran   the holy text of Islam

madrasa   Islamic school with instruction based on the Koran

militant   a person who uses aggressive methods to advance a cause

mujahideen   resistance fighters in Afghanistan who opposed the Soviet invasion and occupation after 1979

narcotic   an addictive drug that may make the user sleepy

North Atlantic Treaty Organization (NATO)   military alliance set up in 1949 during the Cold War to stop Soviet communist power expanding in Europe

Northern Alliance   fighters who opposed the Taliban in Afghanistan, mostly from the north and west of the country

Pashtun   ethnic group living in both Afghanistan and Pakistan, typically rural and conservative

Predator drone   pilotless plane that flies slowly, scanning the ground with a digital TV camera. It can also fire missiles.

sharia   Islamic law governing religious and non-religious life

Shia   the smaller of the two main branches of Islam. Shia Muslims regard Ali, the fourth caliph, as Muhammad's first true successor. Iran is a Shia state.

Soviet Union   also known as the Union of Soviet Socialist Republics (USSR), a communist state that existed from 1917 until the early 1990s, when Russia and other Soviet republics abandoned communism and formed independent governments

Sunni   the biggest branch of Islam (90 per cent of all Muslims), which follows the practices handed down by the first three successors of the Prophet Muhammad. Most Afghans are Sunni.

Tajik   ethnic group; people who live in northern Afghanistan and Tajikistan

Taliban   ultra-strict and conservative Islamist group that came to power in Afghanistan in the 1990s

Uzbek   ethnic group; people who live in northern Afghanistan and Uzbekistan

Further Information

BOOKS

FOR CHILDREN

Nicola Barber, *Changing World, Afghanistan* (Watts, 2008)

David Downing, *Witness to History: Afghanistan* (Heinemann Library, 2004)

Lisa Firth, *The Terrorism Problem* (Independence Educational Publishers, 2008)

Nikki Van der Gaag, *World in Focus: Afghanistan* (Wayland, 2009)

FOR OLDER READERS AND TEACHERS

Alison Behnke, *Afghanistan in Pictures* (Lerner Publishing Group, 2003)

Khalid Hosseini, *The Kite Runner* (Bloomsbury, 2003)

David Loyn, *Butcher and Bolt* (Hutchinson, 2008)

Lloyd Pettiford and David Harding, *Terrorism* (Arcturus, 2003)

Ahmed Rashid, *Taliban: Islam, Oil and the New Great Game in Central Asia* (IB Tauris & Co Ltd, 2008)

Åsne Seierstad, *The Bookseller of Kabul* (Little Brown, 2003)

Saira Shah, *The Storyteller's Daughter* (Michael Joseph, 2003)

WEBSITES

www.cbc.ca/news/viewpoint/vp_sanders – a soldier's diary from Afghanistan

http://www.jfcbs.nato.int/ – NATO website

http://news.bbc.co.uk/1/hi/world/south_asia/country_profiles/1162668.stm – general information about Afghanistan

http://news.bbc.co.uk/1/hi/world/south_asia/7741767.stm – information in graphics about Afghanistan

http://news.bbc.co.uk/1/hi/in_depth/south_asia/afghanistan_pakistan/default.stm – information about the Taliban conflict

http://www.bbc.co.uk/religion/religions/islam/subdivisions/sunnishia_1.shtml – page on the BBC website that explains the differences between Sunni and Shia Muslims

Index

Numbers in **bold** refer to photographs.

9/11 attacks 9, 12–13, **12**, **13**, 15, 21, 36, 40

Achakzai, Sitara 43, **43**
Afghan national army 18, 19, 22, 28, 30, 32, 33, 38, 39, 42, 44
aid 19, 22, 23, 26, 28, 34, 41, 44, 45
air strikes 14, **14**, 15, 18, 23, 38, **38**, 42–43, **42**
Al-Jazeera 29
al-Qaeda 9, 10, 11, 12, 15, 16, 17, 18, 21, 23, 29, 36, 37, 38, 40, 41, 47
Amanullah Shah 5
Amin, Hafizullah 6, 7
Anti-Terrorism Act (US) 13
assassinations 5, 12, 13, 24, **24**, 25, 36, 37, 39

Bhutto, Benazir 36, 37, **37**, 39
bin Laden, Osama 8, 9, 11, 12, 14, 15, 16, 18–19, **18**, 29, 36–37, 46
Britain 4, 12, 21, 26, 29
British troops 14, 18, 23, 26, **27**, 29, 32, 34, **34**, 37
burkas 10, **11**, 47
Bush, George W 11, 12, 13, **13**, 28, 46

Central Intelligence Agency (CIA) **8**, 17, 24, 37, 47
Cheney, Dick 20, 34
Chinook helicopters **23**, 30, **30**, 31
civilian casualties 15, 23, 30, 33, 42–43, **42**, 45
coalition troops 13, 14, 15, 17, 18, 19, 22, 26, 30, 32, 33, 35, 41, **41**, 42, 44, 45, 47
Cold War 6, 47
communism 5, 6, 7, 8, 47
cruise missiles 11, 15, 47

Dadullah 34, 35
Daud Khan 5, 6, 7
Dostum, Abdul Rashid 10, 16

education 10, 11, 22, 27, 28, 32, 33, **33**
elections 28–29, **28**
exit strategy 44–45
extraordinary rendition 17, 47

friendly fire 24, 25

Gorbachev, Mikhail 8, 9
Guantánamo Bay 17, 20–21, **20**, **21**, 45
guerrillas **10**, 16, 47

Hazaras 4, 10, 47
Helmand **4**, 10, 32, 34, **34**
Herat 4, **4**, 10
heroin 24, 25, 47
hostages 34–35, 38

India 4, **4**, 5, 10, 14, 40, 41
insurgents 22, 32, 33, 36, 44, 47
International Security Assistance Force (ISAF) 19, 22, 24, **24**, 26–27, **26**, 28, 32, 42, 44, 47
Inter-Services Intelligence (ISI) **8**, 28, 38, 39, 41
Iran **4**, 8, 10, 36
Iraq War 26, 28, 31, 36, 41
Islam 5, 7, 8, 10, 16, 17, 20, 22, 28, 41
    Shia Muslims 4, 47
    Sunni Muslims 4, 47

jihad 10, 47

Kabul 4, **4**, 5, **6**, 7, **7**, 9, **9**, 10, 11, 13, 14, 16, **16**, 17, 20, 24, 26, **26**, 27, **27**, 33, 40
Kamal, Babrak 6, 7, 8, 9
Kandahar 4, **4**, 10, 16, 24, 25, **31**, 32, 36, **36**, 40, **40**, 43, **43**
Karzai, Hamid 17, 19, 22, 23, 24, 25, 28, 29, **29**, 35, 36, 37, 38, 39, **39**, 42, 43, 46

madrasas 17, 47
Massoud, Ahmad Shah 8, 10, **10**, 12, 13, 16, 46
Mastrogiacomo, Daniele 34, **35**
Mazar-e Sharif 4, **4**, 16, 17, **17**
McChrystal, Stanley 44, **44**, 45, 46
Mohammed, Khalid Sheikh 20–21
mujahideen 8–9, **8**, 10, 18, 37, 47
Musharraf, Pervez 15, 36, 39, **39**, 46

Nadir Shah 4, 5
Najibullah, Mohammed 8, 9, 10, 11
North Atlantic Treaty Organisation (NATO) 13, 26–27, 30, 32, 34, 35, 41, 42, 44, 47
Northern Alliance 10, **10**, 11, 12, 13, 14, 16–17, **16**, 22, 40, 47

Obama, Barack 21, 44, **44**, 45, 46
Omar, Mohammed 8, 10, 13, 16, 35, 43, 44, 46
Operation Achilles 34–35
Operation Enduring Freedom 14–15, **14**, **15**, 27
Operation Mountain Thrust 32–33

Pakistan **4**, 5, 6, 8, 9, 10, 14, 15, 17, 18, 21, 23, 29, 33, 36, 37, 39, 40, 41, 44, 45, **45**
    border 5, 6, 14, 29, 38–39, 40
Pashtuns 4, 5, **5**, 6, 8, 14, 24, 38, 42, 47
Petraeus, David 36, 43
poppy-growing 24, 25, **25**
Predator drones 14, 15, 18, 47
protests 20, **21**, 38, 39, 40, **43**

Qadir, Haji Abdul 24, **24**, 25

Rabbani, Burhanuddin 8, 9, 10, 12, 46
Rawalpindi, Treaty of 4, 5
reconstruction 17, 19, 22, 23, 26, 28, 33
refugees 8, 13, 19, 22, **22**, 45, **45**
Rumsfeld, Donald 15, 33

sharia law 7, 47
Soviet Union (USSR) 5, 6–7, 8, 47
    troops **6**, 7, 8–9, **9**, 16, 18
suicide bombers 9, 29, 36–37, **36**, **37**, 40, 41, 43
Swat Valley 45, **45**

Tajiks 4, 6, 10, 16, 47
Taliban 8, 9, 10–11, 12, 13, 14, 15, **15**, 16, 17, **17**, 18, 22, 23, 24, 25, 26, 28, 29, 30, 31, 32, 33, 34, 35, 36, 37, 38, 39, 40, 41, 42, 43, 44, 45, 47
    prisoners **17**, 35, 38, 40
Taraki, Nur Mohammad 6–7
terror attacks 9, 11, 12–13, 15, 17, 21, 29, 36–37, 40, 41
Tora Bora caves **4**, 18, 19, **19**,
torture 20, 21
training camps 11, 12, 17, 21, 29

United Nations (UN) 9, 19, 26, 36, 42, 43
United States 6, 7, 8, 9, 10, 11, 12, 13, 14, 16, 25, 26, 27, 28, 36, 44
    troops 14, 15, **15**, 18, 19, 23, 26, 28, 30, 36, 38, 39, 41, **41**
Uruzgan **4**, 23, 32
Uzbeks 4, 10, 47

war on terror 12, 13, 40
water boarding 20
weapons **5**, 8, **8**, 26, 28, 30, 34, 36, 38, 40
    of mass destruction (WMDs) 26
women 10–11, **11**, 28, 42, 43

Zahir Shah 4, 5, 22, 23, **29**
Zardari, Asif Ali **37**, 39